D0594137

The Vietnam War

Katie Daynes

Designed by Karen Tomlins

History consultant: Professor O. A. Westad
Cold War Studies Centre
London School of Economics and Political Science

Reading consultant: Alison Kelly, Roehampton University

Edited by Jane Chisholm
Illustrated by Emmanuel Cerisier
Photographic manipulation: Keith Furnival
Photo research by Ruth King, with special thanks to Doug Niven

First published in 2008 by Usborne Publishing Ltd., Usborne House,
83-85 Saffron Hill, London, EC1N 8RT, England. www.usborne.com

Internet links
You can find out more about the Vietnam War
by going to the Usborne Quicklinks Website
at **www.usborne-quicklinks.com**
and typing in the keywords
Vietnam War.

CONTENTS

THIS PHOTO, TAKEN IN 1968, SHOWS
A VIETNAMESE FIGHTER ADVANCING
THROUGH THE JUNGLE.

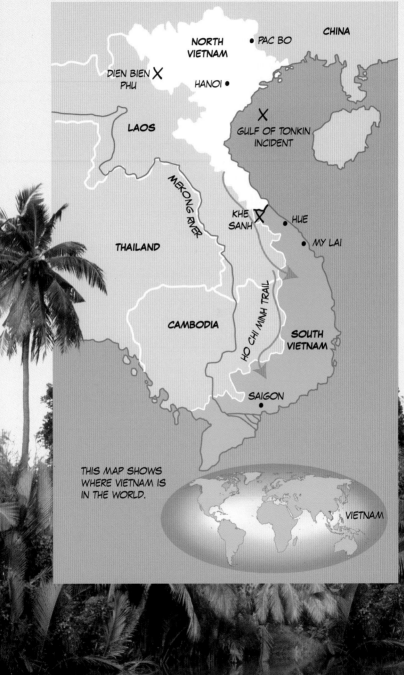

A MAP OF EASTERN ASIA, 1954-1975

CHINA

NORTH VIETNAM

• PAC BO

DIEN BIEN PHU ✕

HANOI •

LAOS

✕
GULF OF TONKIN INCIDENT

MEKONG RIVER

KHE SANH ✕ • HUE

THAILAND

• MY LAI

HO CHI MINH TRAIL

CAMBODIA

SOUTH VIETNAM

SAIGON •

THIS MAP SHOWS WHERE VIETNAM IS IN THE WORLD.

VIETNAM

INTRODUCTION

Vietnam lies in an S-shape down the eastern side of Asia, with China to the north, Laos and Cambodia to the west and the South China Sea to the east. Its towns are rich with ancient temples and palaces, stunning beaches line the coast, and incredible rock formations rise out of the sea.

But inland there's a dense, forbidding jungle that hides a dark and bloody history, overgrown yet not forgotten.

PALM TREES LINE THE MEKONG RIVER AS IT SNAKES ITS WAY THROUGH THE VIETNAMESE JUNGLE TO THE SEA.

CHAPTER 1

HO CHI MINH

In the 1930s, there were demonstrations across Vietnam, with poor farmers protesting against crippling taxes. Vietnam had been ruled by France for over 60 years, against the will of its people. Now, as the peasants grew more restless and frustrated, the French authorities were becoming stricter. They banned all public meetings, stopped people from leaving their district without the right paperwork, and arrested anyone acting suspiciously.

IN THE 1930S, THE MAJORITY OF VIETNAMESE PEOPLE LIVED BY FARMING RICE FIELDS, LIKE THIS ONE.

Meanwhile, in nearby China, one man was keeping a close eye on his homeland. His real name was Nguyen That Thanh, but he later called himself Ho Chi Minh, meaning "he who enlightens" in Vietnamese.

Ho had lived abroad for 30 years. On his travels he had learned about communism – the idea that property should be shared equally among people. He longed for the Vietnamese to share Vietnam, instead of being bullied by foreigners. And he thought communism had the answer: peasants should rise up in a glorious revolution and take control – by force if necessary.

Ho's hopes for his country were shared by Vo Nguyen Giap, a fellow Vietnamese living in China. They were both members of the Indochina Communist Party (ICP), which aimed to overthrow the French and make Vietnam independent. The party was recruiting members all over Vietnam, by smuggling leaflets into the country and holding secret meetings in villages and factories.

VO NGUYEN GIAP (TOP LEFT) AND HO CHI MINH (TOP RIGHT) WORKED CLOSELY TOGETHER FOR YEARS. HERE THEY'RE PLANNING A MILITARY CAMPAIGN IN 1950.

Ho wanted to return to Vietnam to lead an uprising, but the French knew he meant trouble and would instantly arrest him. So he had to wait for the right opportunity.

***

In 1939, the Second World War broke out. Germany invaded France and Japan attacked French bases in Vietnam. During the confusion that followed, Ho managed to sneak back into his country and set up the ICP headquarters at a place called Pac Bo, in a cave surrounded by jungle.

Ho then created the League for the Independence of Vietnam, known as the Viet Minh, with Vo Nguyen Giap in charge. Their idea was to send small groups of Viet Minh fighters all over the country to fight both the French and the Japanese. The fighters were taught 'guerrilla' tactics, such as ambushes and raids, to surprise and defeat the enemy.

The Americans and the Chinese were also at war with Japan. They offered to help the Viet Minh by giving them weapons and financial aid.

Then, in 1945, the United States dropped two devastating nuclear bombs on major cities in Japan. Thousands of Japanese people were killed, Japan surrendered and the Second World War drew to a close.

As soon as Ho heard the news, he appealed to the Vietnamese people to rise in revolution. He wanted them to act quickly, before the French had a chance to regain control. Across the north of Vietnam, the Viet Minh took control of government and police buildings. They renamed the country the Democratic Republic of Vietnam, chose a new national flag – red with a gold star – and declared Ho Chi Minh their president.

Two weeks later, Ho stood in front of a crowd in the northern city of Hanoi and read out the Vietnamese Declaration of Independence. He borrowed phrases from both the American Declaration of Independence and the Declaration of the French Revolution.

"All men are born free and with equal rights," cried Ho, "and must always remain free and have equal rights." He argued that for 80 years the French had denied the Vietnamese people those rights.

"They have built more prisons than schools," he shouted to the crowd. "They have robbed us of our rice fields, our mines, our forests, and our raw materials... Vietnam has the right to be a free and independent country, and in fact is so already."

Ho's words filled his followers with confidence, but the struggle for independence had a long way to go.

HO CHI MINH MADE PEOPLE IN VIETNAM BELIEVE THAT INDEPENDENCE WAS POSSIBLE. HERE, FELLOW COMMUNISTS DEMONSTRATE THEIR SUPPORT.

In September 1945, French troops, captured by the Japanese during the Second World War, were released from prison. They swiftly won control of towns in southern Vietnam and forced the Viet Minh to retreat into the jungle. Meanwhile, more French troops were arriving in the north. It wasn't long before clashes between the French and the Viet Minh exploded into a full-scale war.

At first, the French had the upper hand. They had superior weapons, lots more troops and the support of many Vietnamese who didn't want their country ruled by communists.

But, as the weeks, months and years went by, the Viet Minh still didn't surrender.

They continued their guerrilla tactics, wearing down the French troops by attacking them when they least expected.

Ho Chi Minh found powerful allies in nearby communist countries, China and the Soviet Union. As interest in the war waned in faraway France, the Viet Minh became stronger.

In 1954, the Viet Minh fought a major battle at the town of Dien Bien Phu. Equipped with Chinese weapons and led by Vo Nguyen Giap, they won an overwhelming victory. This was the last straw for the French. They reluctantly admitted defeat and prepared to leave.

VIETNAMESE SOLDIERS ATTACK A FRENCH MILITARY BASE DURING THE BATTLE AT DIEN BIEN PHU. THE FIGHTING LASTED FOR 56 DAYS.

CHAPTER 2

FIGHTING COMMUNISM

The French finally left Vietnam in 1954. After almost a century of colonial rule, Ho Chi Minh was poised to take control. But the success of the communist Viet Minh had set off warning bells in other corners of the world. Ever since the Russian Revolution in 1917, the threat of communism had struck fear in the hearts of many.

The idea of communism was to give everyone equal rights and opportunities. But the communist government in Russia, renamed the Soviet Union in 1922, had turned out to be brutal and oppressive.

By the end of the Second World War, the world had two great superpowers – the United States and the Soviet Union. Both countries had nuclear bombs so powerful they could wipe out whole cities... and they were fierce rivals.

The United States was watching the Soviet leader, Stalin, with growing distrust. Already, he had imposed communism on five countries in eastern Europe. Now he was encouraging communists in other countries to rise up and take control.

YOUNG COMMUNISTS CARRY A HUGE PORTRAIT OF THEIR LEADER, STALIN, ON A PARADE.

A WORLD MAP SHOWING THE SPREAD OF COMMUNISM

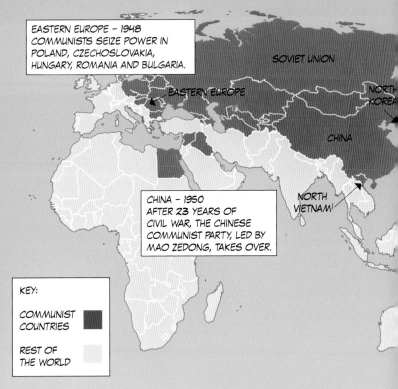

EASTERN EUROPE – 1948
COMMUNISTS SEIZE POWER IN
POLAND, CZECHOSLOVAKIA,
HUNGARY, ROMANIA AND BULGARIA.

SOVIET UNION

EASTERN EUROPE

NORTH KOREA

CHINA

CHINA – 1950
AFTER 23 YEARS OF
CIVIL WAR, THE CHINESE
COMMUNIST PARTY, LED BY
MAO ZEDONG, TAKES OVER.

NORTH VIETNAM

KEY:

COMMUNIST
COUNTRIES

REST OF
THE WORLD

The US and other western governments feared
what they called the domino effect. They believed
that if a few countries fell to communism, it could
spread like a disease around the world. But if the
US attacked the Soviet Union directly, they risked
sparking off a third World War. So, instead, they
decided to give support to other countries in their
fights against communism.

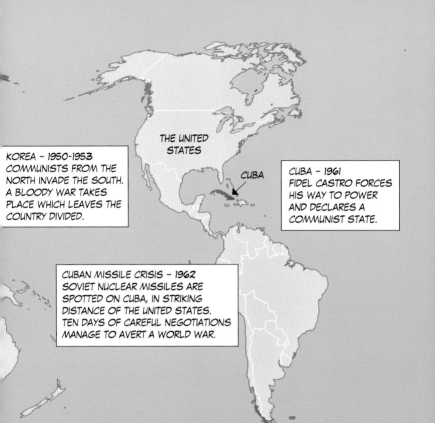

KOREA – 1950-1953
COMMUNISTS FROM THE
NORTH INVADE THE SOUTH.
A BLOODY WAR TAKES
PLACE WHICH LEAVES THE
COUNTRY DIVIDED.

THE UNITED
STATES

CUBA

CUBA – 1961
FIDEL CASTRO FORCES
HIS WAY TO POWER
AND DECLARES A
COMMUNIST STATE.

CUBAN MISSILE CRISIS – 1962
SOVIET NUCLEAR MISSILES ARE
SPOTTED ON CUBA, IN STRIKING
DISTANCE OF THE UNITED STATES.
TEN DAYS OF CAREFUL NEGOTIATIONS
MANAGE TO AVERT A WORLD WAR.

In July 1954, a conference was held in
Switzerland to decide Vietnam's future. The Viet
Minh reluctantly agreed that Vietnam should be
temporarily split in two, with them taking control
of the north. Almost a million Vietnamese then
fled from North Vietnam and a fervent anti-
communist, Ngo Dihn Diem, proclaimed himself
president of South Vietnam.

An election to unite the country was scheduled for 1956. But Diem refused to take part, because he was sure the Viet Minh would win. The Americans offered Diem their full support. They gave him money and promised him military aid, in order to strengthen South Vietnam against a possible invasion from the communist North.

Meanwhile, Diem ordered the arrest of any suspected communists. Thousands fled the South to avoid being tortured or killed, while others went into hiding in rural areas.

Back in Hanoi, Ho Chi Minh heard what Diem was doing and he was furious. He responded by instructing South Vietnamese communists to make surprise attacks against their government. In the following months, the communists managed to assassinate hundreds of Diem's officials.

Soon it wasn't just the communists rebelling against Diem's government, but others too who wanted their country reunited. Under the direction of Ho Chi Minh, a new party was created: the NLF (National Liberation Front for South Vietnam). The NLF led uprisings in many villages and took over large rural areas. Both the Soviet Union and China announced their approval.

In the United States, President John F. Kennedy followed the NLF's progress anxiously. South Vietnam was swiftly becoming the main battlefield in a global war against communism. In 1961, Kennedy sent 400 Special Forces troops to act as advisors to Diem's army. Their job was to train South Vietnamese soldiers to fight against the NLF.

A LIEUTENANT FROM THE US SPECIAL FORCES INSTRUCTS A GROUP OF SOUTH VIETNAMESE ON HOW TO USE A BAYONET.

BUDDHIST LEADER, THICH TRI QUANG (LEFT), LEADS A DEMONSTRATION ON
THE STREETS OF SAIGON AGAINST THE SOUTH VIETNAMESE GOVERNMENT.

But it was becoming clear that the US had
backed the wrong man. Diem's rule was aggressive
and corrupt. He gave the best jobs to his relatives
and the best deals to people who shared his
Catholic faith.

Diem's policies discriminated against both
communists and Buddhists. Since Buddhism was
Vietnam's main religion, this sparked a lot of
resentment. Some Buddhist monks even set fire
to themselves in protest, then sat calmly as they
burned to death. The scenes provoked outrage
around the world.

President Kennedy criticized Diem on television, and the South Vietnamese army decided to take matters into their own hands. They overthrew Diem's government and executed him and his brother.

Only three weeks later, Kennedy was dead too – assassinated by a gunman. The new president, Lyndon B. Johnson, wanted to stand firm against the communists. But he couldn't authorize military action without an official reason – and so far the Americans hadn't come under attack.

On August 4th, 1964, President Johnson received reports that the North Vietnamese had fired at US warships in the Gulf of Tonkin. That same week, the US passed a new law giving the president powers to fight back. Johnson immediately ordered air strikes on North Vietnamese ships and increased the number of US advisors in South Vietnam.

THE NAVY DESTROYER, USS MADDOX,
WAS ONE OF THE US SHIPS INVOLVED
IN THE GULF OF TONKIN INCIDENT.

HOW THE TONKIN INCIDENT LED TO MILITARY ACTION

American military leaders called for more troops and bombing campaigns, but Johnson was reluctant. "There is no place in today's world for weakness," he told his people. "But there is also no place in today's world for recklessness."

In November 1964 Johnson was elected president again, but it took several more attacks on American troops before he committed to fighting in Vietnam.

On the evening of February 7th 1965, hundreds of NLF fighters crept up on a US airbase and bombarded 400 sleeping American soldiers. Seven Americans died and 100 were wounded.

When Johnson heard about the attack, his mind was made up. "They are killing our men while they are asleep at night," he exclaimed. "I can't ask American soldiers to continue to fight with one hand behind their backs."

JOHNSON ORDERED A LONG SERIES OF BOMBINGS IN NORTH VIETNAM. TARGETS INCLUDED THIS TORPEDO BOAT, BOMBED ON MAY 14TH 1965.

So, he summoned his military leaders and ordered a two-pronged attack: a major bombing campaign against North Vietnam, and the departure of four US military ships and thousands of troops for South Vietnam.

The American war in Vietnam was now underway. Before long, Australia, New Zealand and South Korea sent troops as well, to join the fight against communism.

AMERICAN TROOPS REACH THE VIETNAMESE SHORE AND RUN FOR COVER.

CHAPTER 3

A JUNGLE WAR

For several years, an undercover operation had been taking place deep in the South Vietnamese jungle. The NLF were infiltrating village after village.

They had a cunning strategy. By moving around in small groups and talking with people in places they knew, they learned about local problems and concerns. Without ever mentioning communism, they encouraged people to turn against the government.

APPROACHING BY BOAT, NLF GUERRILLAS AND LOCAL FARMERS ATTACK A GROUP OF SOUTH VIETNAMESE SOLDIERS.

In 1963, the North Vietnamese had sent a colonel named Bui Tin to report on the NLF's progress. To get into the country secretly, he used an extensive network of jungle paths, that became known as the Ho Chi Minh trail. It was a gruelling six-month trek, through steamy rainforest, crawling with deadly creatures.

When Colonel Bui Tin finally returned, he brought with him bad news. The NLF urgently needed support or they would lose their guerrilla war. The North Vietnamese government responded instantly. They sent engineers to construct roads and bridges along the Ho Chi Minh trail. Fuel depots, hospitals and army camps were built – underground, so they couldn't be spotted from the air.

Within a year, the trail had become an efficient supply route. The Soviets and Chinese donated trucks, which transported a steady flow of weapons, equipment and people into South Vietnam. By the time the American troops landed in 1965, the NLF and the North Vietnamese Army (NVA) were already waiting.

Their first major clash came after a surprise attack by the NVA on an American army base.

NLF GUERRILLAS TRANSPORT FOOD AND AMMUNITION DOWN PART OF THE HO CHI MINH TRAIL.

As the North Vietnamese retreated into the jungle, the American commander, General William Westmoreland, ordered his helicopters to follow.

The NVA were regrouping in an area known as the Ia Drang valley, when they heard a drone of helicopter blades and felt the air around them being sucked away. The helicopters hovered dangerously low and dozens of US soldiers scrambled out. The NVA opened fire and a fierce battle began.

A US MACHINE GUNNER MONITORS THE VIETNAMESE COUNTRYSIDE FROM A HELICOPTER.

The North Vietnamese had more troops, but the American aircraft had heavy firepower. Eventually the Vietnamese turned and fled. Around 300 American troops lost their lives, but they had killed an estimated 1,200 Vietnamese. Westmoreland hailed it a victory.

For Ho Chi Minh and General Giap, the Battle of Ia Drang confirmed what they already knew: in a straight battle between the two sides, America would always win. Their only chance was to grind down their enemy gradually, until they finally gave up.

Ho took inspiration from the advice of Mao Zedong, the communist leader in China. "The enemy advances, we retreat," he said, "the enemy camps, we harass; the enemy tires, we attack; the enemy retreats, we pursue."

* * *

Many American soldiers knew little about their enemy. They called them the Vietcong – from the local term for Vietnamese communists – and thought of them as a random scattering of untrained peasants, armed with only bows and arrows.

But in fact the Vietcong were highly organized. Each new recruit joined a three-man group, called a cell, which included one experienced fighter. They would operate together for life and become extremely close.

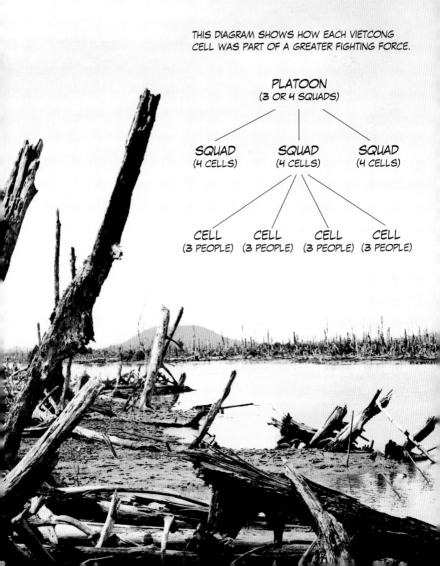

THIS DIAGRAM SHOWS HOW EACH VIETCONG CELL WAS PART OF A GREATER FIGHTING FORCE.

PLATOON
(3 OR 4 SQUADS)

SQUAD
(4 CELLS)

SQUAD
(4 CELLS)

SQUAD
(4 CELLS)

CELL
(3 PEOPLE)

CELL
(3 PEOPLE)

CELL
(3 PEOPLE)

CELL
(3 PEOPLE)

The new recruits were usually peasant farmers, so they were used to backbreaking work and hardship. Many of them were also highly motivated, believing they were fighting a corrupt regime and an aggressive foreign power.

Since 1962, American airmen had been spraying chemicals over the Vietnamese jungles. Their intent was to kill trees and crops, so the Vietcong had nowhere to hide and nothing to eat. Unfortunately, innocent villagers went hungry too.

One chemical, known as Agent Orange, was particularly nasty. Over nine years, it destroyed one-seventh of South Vietnam's vegetation. It was later found to cause cancer and birth defects too.

A VIETNAMESE MAN ROWS THROUGH THE REMAINS OF A MANGROVE FOREST, KILLED OFF BY AGENT ORANGE.

SOUTH VIETNAMESE SOLDIERS GUARD A NEW VILLAGE,
SET UP UNDER THE STRATEGIC HAMLET PROGRAM.

Another American tactic was the Strategic Hamlet program. To prevent peasants from being influenced by the Vietcong, many were moved to new villages controlled by the South Vietnamese army.

But the peasants didn't want to leave their homes. Soldiers ended up moving them by force, then ordering them to dig moats and erect fences around the new village. This increased the peasants' resentment and actually encouraged them to join the Vietcong.

The Vietcong relied heavily on the element of surprise to defeat their enemy. They mostly attacked at night, using a technique known as one slow, four quick (see opposite).

THE VIETCONG ATTACKING TECHNIQUE

ONE SLOW: CAREFUL PREPARATION

FOUR QUICK:

1. ADVANCE QUICKLY

2. ASSAULT QUICKLY

3. CLEAR THE BATTLEFIELD QUICKLY

4. WITHDRAW QUICKLY

THEY GOT AWAY AGAIN!

GRRRR!!

Their orders were to kill as many Americans as possible. The war was unpopular in the United States, they were told, and over time the Americans would give up and go home. If the Vietcong let the war drag on, they believed that ultimately victory would be theirs.

THIS POSTER FROM CHINA CALLS FOR THE AMERICANS TO LEAVE SOUTH VIETNAM.

US ARMY DRAFTEES WORK UP A SWEAT DURING THEIR FIRST WEEK OF TRAINING.

CHAPTER 4

365 DAYS

Across the United States, there were families who lived in fear of "the draft" – a letter summoning young men to become soldiers for a year. While some men relished the idea of being soldiers, others did all they could to escape the draft. Methods of 'draft dodging' included going to college, moving to Canada, or even feigning an illness so they failed the medical examination. But the majority were sent to army camps around the US to begin their military training.

When draftees entered the armed forces, they were issued with a uniform and their heads were shaved. They slept in dormitories and were woken at the crack of dawn to go for a run, clean the toilets, or perform any command their sergeant yelled at them.

New recruits were taught how to march in formation, use a gun and do guard duty. Above all, they learned obedience. Most learned it the hard way. A scuffed shoe or a missing button was punished by a dozen press-ups and public humiliation.

The recruits dressed in camouflage, slid on their bellies through swamps, ran for miles with heavy packs on their backs... but nothing could prepare them for what lay ahead.

Each week, a plane packed with young soldiers touched down at the US army base in Vietnam. As they stepped off their air-conditioned plane, it felt like entering a steaming hot sauna. They would have to endure this heat for 365 days, unless injury or death took them home sooner.

New arrivals were given a series of talks, describing the geography of Vietnam and the nature of the war. At each new revelation, many faces lengthened with anxiety.

THIS PHOTO, TAKEN IN THE UNITED STATES, SHOWS AMERICAN SOLDIERS TRAINING IN A MOCK VIETCONG VILLAGE.

AN ARMY SERGEANT EXPLAINS WHAT THE WAR IS REALLY LIKE

THERE IS NO FRONT LINE... OR RATHER THE FRONT LINE IS EVERYWHERE.

MUCH OF THE COUNTRY IS DENSE JUNGLE, HOME TO LEECHES, SCORPIONS, MOSQUITOS AND POISONOUS SNAKES.

THE NORTH VIETNAMESE USE SECRET PATHS TO ENTER SOUTH VIETNAM AT ANY TIME.

THE VIETCONG – WHO WE CALL THE VC OR CHARLIE – ARE HERE ALREADY. LOOK OUT FOR THE GUYS IN BLACK PYJAMAS...

...THOUGH THEY OFTEN DISGUISE THEMSELVES AS CIVILIANS.

The good news for the American soldiers was that the US had overwhelming firepower and a new weapon hardly used in any other war – the helicopter.

Soon after arriving, soldiers were flown to smaller, more remote bases, some consisting of only a bunker, a helipad and a cluster of tents. For protection, they were surrounded by a few rolls of wire and holes in the ground – known as fox holes – where soldiers hid to keep guard. Squads of eight men, led by a sergeant, were sent out on foot patrol for several days at a time.

US SOLDIERS ON FOOT PATROL MAKE THEIR WAY THROUGH A SWAMP.

It was heavy work in the stuffy heat. Soldiers carried their own kit in a large backpack. They soon earned themselves the nickname 'grunts' because of the noise they made struggling under the weight of their packs.

Noise was a dangerous giveaway in the jungle. The slightest cough would alert the Vietcong to enemy presence. Soldiers hated it when a new guy joined their squad. He could put everyone's lives in danger just by speaking.

And yet the jungle was never silent. Leaves rustled in the canopy, small creatures scampered through the undergrowth, insects droned relentlessly. There was the croak of a frog, the chatter of a monkey, the hoot of an owl...

In the dark of night, these noises seemed louder and more sinister. Soldiers spent sleepless nights waiting to ambush the Vietcong. They positioned themselves in an L-shape, with a machine-gunner facing up the trail and the other men spaced out in a line behind. On a successful night they might capture a band of guerrillas. But more often they just sat still as stones, monsoon rain streaming down their faces, until dawn broke and they wandered wearily back to their base.

Many troops never even saw the Vietcong. They were shot at and plagued by booby traps, but rarely came face to face with the enemy.

A GROUP OF VIETCONG CREEP UP ON A US BASE IN THE DEAD OF NIGHT.

The Vietcong's ability simply to vanish left the soldiers feeling confused and unnerved. It wasn't until 1966 that they discovered where the Vietcong went...

FOR TWO DAYS, AUSTRALIAN TROOPS HAD BEEN SEARCHING THE JUNGLE FOR THE VIETCONG HEADQUARTERS, BUT HAD FOUND NOTHING...

...UNTIL SERGEANT STEWART GREEN STEPPED ON SOMETHING SHARP.

OUCH! WHAT WAS THAT?

GUYS, COME AND SEE THIS!

44

THE TROOPS DISCOVERED THEY WERE STANDING ON A HUGE NETWORK OF TUNNELS, LIKE THIS. THEY USED EXPLOSIVES TO KILL THE VIETCONG HIDING UNDERGROUND.

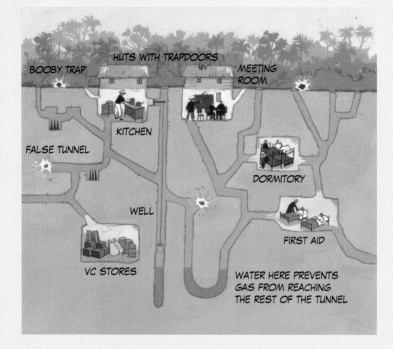

HUTS WITH TRAPDOORS

BOOBY TRAP

MEETING ROOM

KITCHEN

FALSE TUNNEL

DORMITORY

WELL

FIRST AID

VC STORES

WATER HERE PREVENTS GAS FROM REACHING THE REST OF THE TUNNEL

Searching tunnels, and killing or capturing any Vietcong hiding beneath the ground, quickly became a major part of the war.

Small, slim soldiers, nicknamed tunnel rats, were specially chosen for these daunting missions. Their job became increasingly dangerous as the Vietcong added dead ends and booby traps to the tunnel systems.

As the war dragged on, American troops grew tired and wanted to go home to their families. Soldiers would talk about how many days short they were, meaning how many days were left out of their 365 in Vietnam.

The only respite came when troops were allowed on short breaks. It was an opportunity to enjoy the peace and beauty found elsewhere in Vietnam. They lazed on sandy beaches, swam in turquoise seas or headed to the capital, Saigon, where they spent their dollars on having a good time and tried to blank out the haunting horrors of war.

US SOLDIERS ENJOY A BRIEF MOMENT OF PEACE ON A VIETNAMESE BEACH.

A WOUNDED
US SOLDIER IS
AIRLIFTED TO
SAFETY.

CHAPTER 5

THE TET OFFENSIVE

By the end of 1967, there were nearly half a
million US troops in Vietnam and victory was still
not in sight. President Johnson used the high body
count – the number of Vietcong and NVA killed
– to argue that America was winning. But the
number of US casualties was soaring too and the
war was becoming deeply unpopular.

From Hanoi, Ho Chi Minh offered a glimmer
of hope by promising to enter into peace talks so
long as the bombing stopped.

But this was a cunning ploy to put the Americans off their guard. In reality, the communists were planning their biggest offensive yet. So far, the fighting had only taken place in the countryside. Now they wanted to bring it to the cities. The celebration of Tet – the Vietnamese New Year – was the perfect time for a surprise attack.

In previous years, Tet had been marked by a ceasefire. This year, thousands of Vietcong descended on the cities, pretending to visit relatives. They smuggled arms with them, hidden in coffins. As revellers in Saigon set off firecrackers to welcome in the new lunar year, the Vietcong began shooting. They swept through the city, attacking public buildings.

VIETCONG GUERRILLAS STUDY A MAP IN PREPARATION FOR THE TET ATTACKS.

The attacks weren't limited to Saigon. That same night, there were communist uprisings in four other major South Vietnamese cities. Most of the fighting was quickly quelled, but in the old imperial capital, Hue, the communists held out for 25 days.

Over 200 Americans lost their lives in the battle for Hue, along with almost 400 South Vietnamese troops. But the North Vietnamese and Vietcong body count was even higher: over 5,000. After months of very little progress, the US military considered this a victory.

US TROOPS COME UNDER FIRE AS THEY TRY TO FORCE THE VIETCONG OUT OF HUE. THE SOLDIER ON THE LEFT IS RADIOING FOR HELP.

Meanwhile, a major siege was underway at Khe Sanh, a US military base near the border with Laos. Around 4,000 American troops were surrounded by over 20,000 North Vietnamese.

General Westmoreland made the mistake of announcing the importance of Khe Sanh on US television. After that, there was no chance of withdrawing troops without public humiliation.

The communists were delighted. The siege diverted US army attention from their attacks on the cities and made the war even more unpopular in America.

Day after day, the Khe Sanh base was bombarded by rockets and shells. All the Americans could do was sit tight and fire back. No amount of bombing from American aircraft seemed to deter the North Vietnamese.

As the weeks went by, living conditions inside the base became unbearable. Men could hardly sleep for the scream of jets and deafening explosions. They lived in underground bunkers that crawled with rats and stank of dirty bodies. Only a serious injury or death could earn them a flight out of the base.

After 77 days, an overland US relief mission managed to get through. The North Vietnamese retreated and the siege was finally over. By then, the lush hills of Khe Sanh looked more like the dusty surface of the moon. Back in the United States, Westmoreland declared another victory, but this time many people were unconvinced.

The media had become the army's worst enemy. Journalists and TV reporters in Vietnam were giving first-hand accounts of the war, exposing the true extent of the violence to the world. Falling bombs provided some of the most vivid footage. Some were made with napalm – a highly inflammable substance that stuck to everything in sight and burned with an intense heat.

A NAPALM STRIKE EXPLODES IN A FIREBALL CLOSE TO US SOLDIERS.

There were also images of the victims of napalm: screaming villagers running for safety, their whole bodies on fire. Around the world, people condemned the use of these bombs. There were anti-war demonstrations in London, Stockholm, Tokyo, Sydney and other major cities. In America, some young men even burned their army draft papers and many people, including movie stars and politicians, demanded peace.

Wherever President Johnson went, he faced angry protesters chanting anti-war slogans.

"Hey, hey, LBJ. How many kids did you kill today?" shouted hordes of American students.

As a result of all this pressure, Johnson called a stop to the bombings on Hanoi and offered more peace talks. Presidential elections were six months away, but Johnson didn't want to be distracted by an election campaign. Instead, he was determined to give his full attention to creating a lasting peace. So, to the surprise of many, he announced he wouldn't stand as president again.

No American president had ever lost a war. That problem would be passed on to someone else.

CHAPTER 6

GOODBYE VIETNAM

Peace talks with the Vietnamese were always going to be tricky. The different parties couldn't even agree on the shape of the meeting table, and Ho Chi Minh's deteriorating health meant he wouldn't be there to represent the communists.

The talks began in Paris in 1968 and stretched out over several years. The Americans wanted an end to the fighting first and a political solution later. But the North Vietnamese wouldn't stop fighting until they were satisfied they would get their way.

VIETNAMESE AND AMERICAN OFFICIALS MEET FOR PEACE TALKS IN PARIS, 1968.

So the war dragged on and thousands more people were killed.

In 1969, Ho Chi Minh died and Richard Nixon replaced Johnson as the American president. Nixon promised to bring about an end to US involvement in Vietnam. He gradually introduced the policy of Vietnamization – the idea that the South Vietnamese should take over the fighting. The US troops would train them up and give them weapons, then gradually withdraw.

But South Vietnamese soldiers were used to having US support and didn't want to continue alone. At the same time, increasing numbers of US troops refused to take part in a war that

AMERICAN AND SOUTH VIETNAMESE SOLDIERS LISTEN ANXIOUSLY TO A SPEECH MADE BY PRESIDENT NIXON.

CROWDS IN WASHINGTON D.C. PROTEST AGAINST THE
NUMBER OF GIs (US SOLDIERS) KILLED IN VIETNAM.

was so unpopular at home. Now that peace had
been promised, who would want to be the last
soldier to die in Vietnam?

In November 1969, news broke of a horrific
massacre that had been hushed up for over a year.
A group of US soldiers had been sent to My Lai,
a South Vietnamese village where hundreds of
Vietcong were thought to be hiding. Lieutenant
William Calley was in charge of one of the
platoons. For months he had been searching for
Vietcong in the jungle. He had watched as his men
were killed by booby traps and rifle fire. But Calley
had never seen the enemy in the flesh. He was
deeply frustrated and wanted revenge.

TWO FRIGHTENED CHILDREN LIE IN THE AMERICANS' PATH OUTSIDE MY LAI.

At My Lai there were no apparent Vietcong, just women, children and elderly men. But this didn't stop Calley from ordering his men to open fire. They shot anyone who tried to flee, destroyed their huts and crops, rounded up the survivors and herded them into a drainage ditch, then sprayed them with bullets until no one was left alive. Over 150 people were murdered that day.

Lieutenant Calley believed he was doing his job. He saw the women as wives of the Vietcong and their children as future Vietcong fighters. Many of his men boasted about their great victory at My Lai. But when news of the atrocity finally reached the American public, there was outrage.

HOUSES IN MY LAI, SET ALIGHT BY
AMERICAN SOLDIERS, BURN TO ASHES.

Calley was called to Washington, where he thought he would be given a medal. Instead he was arrested and charged with murder. Reports of other atrocities reached the media too. It became increasingly clear that the US had lost its grip on the war.

President Nixon started withdrawing soldiers by the thousands. He widened the peace talks to include China and the Soviet Union, hoping they could persuade North Vietnam to stop fighting.

An agreement was almost reached in 1972, but the South Vietnamese refused to accept North Vietnamese demands. Nixon then ordered a massive bombing campaign on Hanoi. He knew it would be unpopular, but he was still desperately hoping for a victory.

"I would rather be a one-term president," he told a TV audience, "than see America accept its first defeat in its 190-year history."

Thousands of North Vietnamese were killed in these bombings, but still the Hanoi government refused to back down. In the end, the US decided to accept their demands. South Vietnam had no choice but to agree.

A peace agreement was signed in January 1973. It stated that there would be an end to fighting in Vietnam, armies on both sides would keep whatever land they held, US troops would leave Vietnam within 60 days and all prisoners of war would be returned.

For the United States, the war was finally over. Over 58,000 Americans had been killed, about

300,000 had been wounded, billions of dollars had been spent and nothing had been gained. US soldiers who had risked their lives in the jungle received no hero's welcome and very little support or recognition for their service to their country.

But the conflict didn't end there. North and South Vietnam both accused each other of breaking the ceasefire and the fighting continued. China and the Soviet Union resumed their support of North Vietnam, while the South grew weaker as America reduced its aid.

In March 1975, the North Vietnamese launched an offensive to take over the whole country. Within two months, they had swept through the South and surrounded Saigon. The city came under fierce fire. American administrators were evacuated by US helicopters and thousands of South Vietnamese struggled to join them.

VILLAGERS RUN TOWARDS A US HELICOPTER, DESPERATE TO ESCAPE FROM THE ADVANCING NORTH VIETNAMESE ARMY.

NORTH VIETNAMESE TROOPS ENTER SAIGON, APRIL 30TH 1975.

The next day, North Vietnamese tanks drove unopposed through the streets of Saigon. They renamed the capital Ho Chi Minh City, after their great leader. Years of bloody battle and persistence had paid off. The war was over and South Vietnam was theirs.

But it wasn't a happy ending for many South Vietnamese. Thousands were arrested by the communists and sent to camps where they were abused and tortured. Over a million people fled the country and started a new life overseas – mostly in the United States.

Vietnam is still a united, communist country today. Tourists flock to admire its beauty and culture. But the countryside and the people still bear the scars of a long and costly war.

TIMELINE

1939   - Ho Chi Minh returns to Vietnam.

1946   - The French war in Vietnam begins.

1954   - The French are defeated at Dien Bien Phu and decide to withdraw.

1955   - Diem becomes president of South Vietnam. He refuses to hold national elections.

1960   - Kennedy is elected president of the US.
        - The National Liberation Front is formed.

1963   - Assassination of President Kennedy.
        - Diem is overthrown and murdered.

1964   - The Gulf of Tonkin Incident.
        - US President Johnson wins the election.

1965   - The US begins bombing North Vietnam and sends troops to South Vietnam.

1968   - Seige of Khe Sanh and Tet Offensive.
        - My Lai massacre.
        - Paris peace talks begin.

1969   - Nixon replaces Johnson as president.
        - Nixon introduces the Vietnamization policy.
        - Ho Chi Minh dies.
        - Massive anti-war demonstrations take place.

1973   - A ceasefire is signed in Paris.
        - The last American troops leave Vietnam.

1974   - Vietnamese communists resume fighting.

1975   - South Vietnam falls to the communists.

TWO VIETNAMESE WOMEN MOURN
THEIR RELATIVES AT A MILITARY
CEMETERY IN 1975.

INDEX

ACKNOWLEDGEMENTS

© **ASSOCIATED PRESS** p21, p32, p47, pp52-53;
© **CORBIS** pp4-5 (Owen Franken), pp12-13 (Dien Bien Phu Museum/ Reuters), pp14-15 (Bettman), p19 (Bettman), p20 (Bettman), p23 (Hulton-Deutsch Collection), p28 (Bettman), p35 (Leif Skoogfors), p46, pp50-51, p55, p56 (Bettman), p57 (JP Laffont/Sygma), pp60-61 (Nik Wheeler), p62 (Jacques Pavlovsky/ Sygma); © **Getty Images** cover and p1 (Larry Burrows/Time & Life Pictures), pp2-3 (Three Lions/Hulton Archive), p8, p11 (AFP), pp24-25 (Paul Schutzer/Time & Life Pictures), pp36-37 (Lynn Pelham/Time & Life Pictures), p58, p59 (Ronald S. Haeberle/Time & Life Pictures), p63 (Francoise Demulder/AFP); © **Le Minh Truong** pp30-31; © **Ly Way** p42; © **National Geographic Images** pp6-7 (Steve Raymer); © **TopFoto** pp40-41; © **Vietnam News Agency** p25 (Mai Loc), pp26-27 (Dinh Thuy); © **Vo Anh Khanh** p48;
with permission from IWM p34**

Some of the photographs in this book were originally black and white and have been digitally tinted by Usborne Publishing.

Every effort has been made to trace and acknowledge ownership of copyright. The publishers offer to rectify any omissions in future editions, following notification.